MEL BAY PRESENTS

JAZZ Guitar Ensembles | Level 3

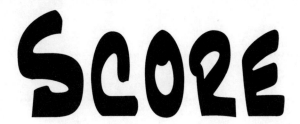

SCORE

Chris Buzzelli

Dave Frackenpohl

Barry Greene

Adrian Ingram

Steve Schenkel

1 2 3 4 5 6 7 8 9 0

© 2004 BY MEL BAY PUBLICATIONS, INC., PACIFIC, MO 63069.

Visit us on the Web at www.melbay.com — E-mail us at email@melbay.com

Table of Contents

Bossa Blue
For Four Guitars

Steve Schenkel

4

D.C. AL CODA

CODA ⊕

5

CARNIVAL
FOR FIVE GUITARS

Adrian Ingram

7

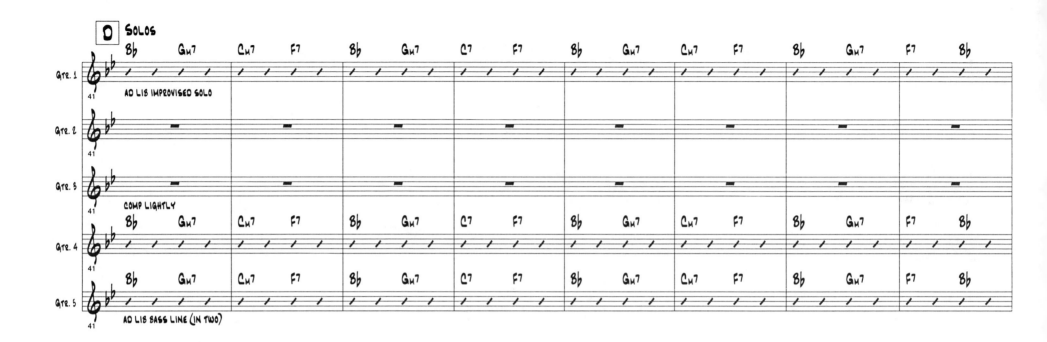

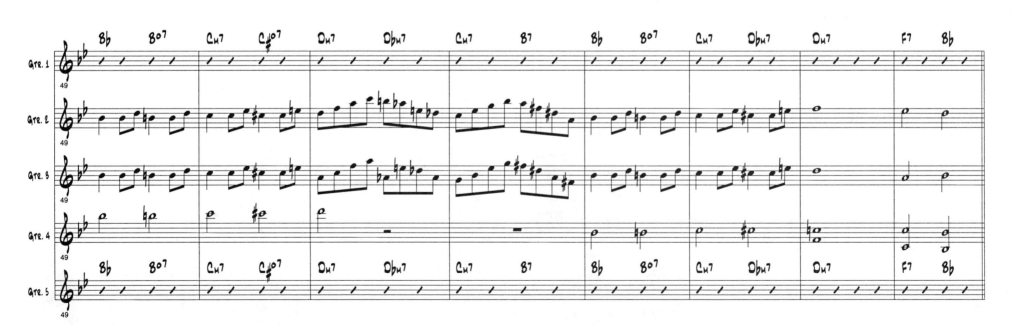

9

11

The Loose Apaloosa

For Five Guitars

Chris Buzzelli

12

13

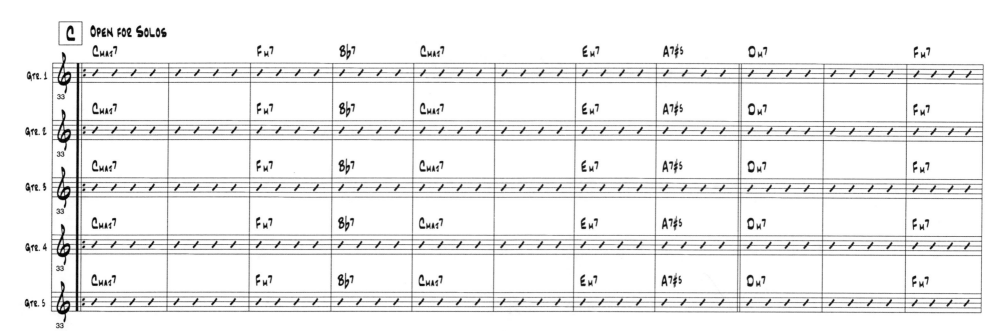

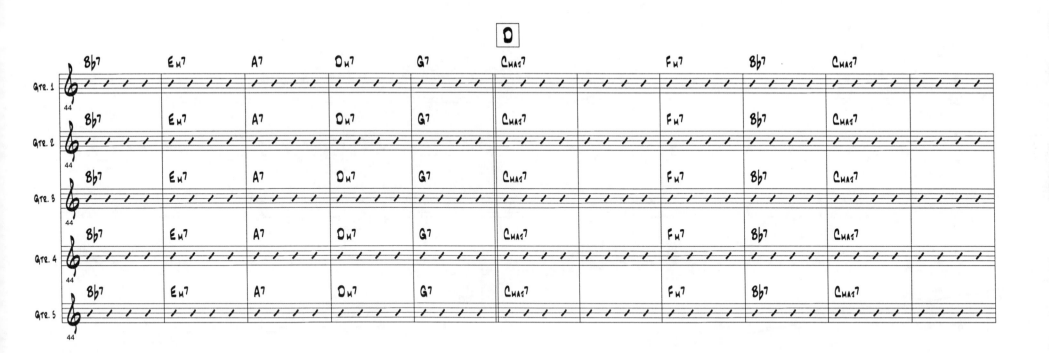

15

Sand Bag
For Five Guitars

Dave Frackenpohl

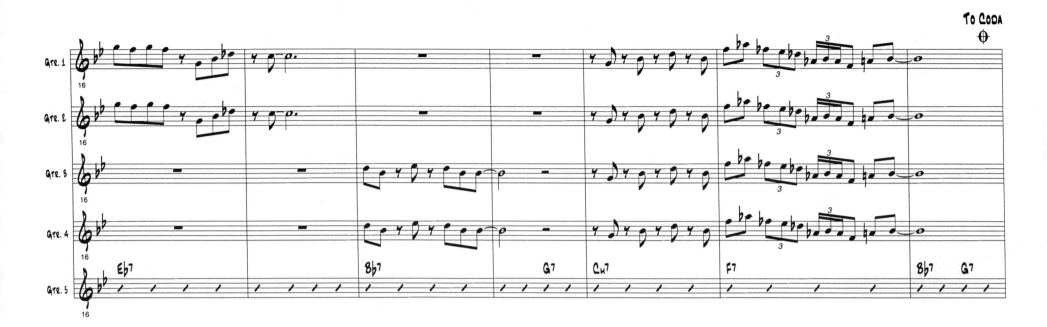

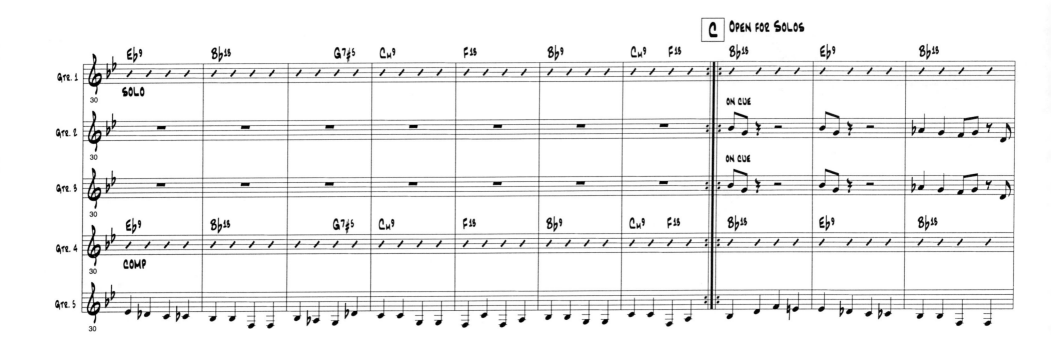

22

D.S. AL CODA
(PLAY SECTION "A" BOTH TIMES)

Voodoo
For Five Guitars

Barry Greene

27

FINE

28

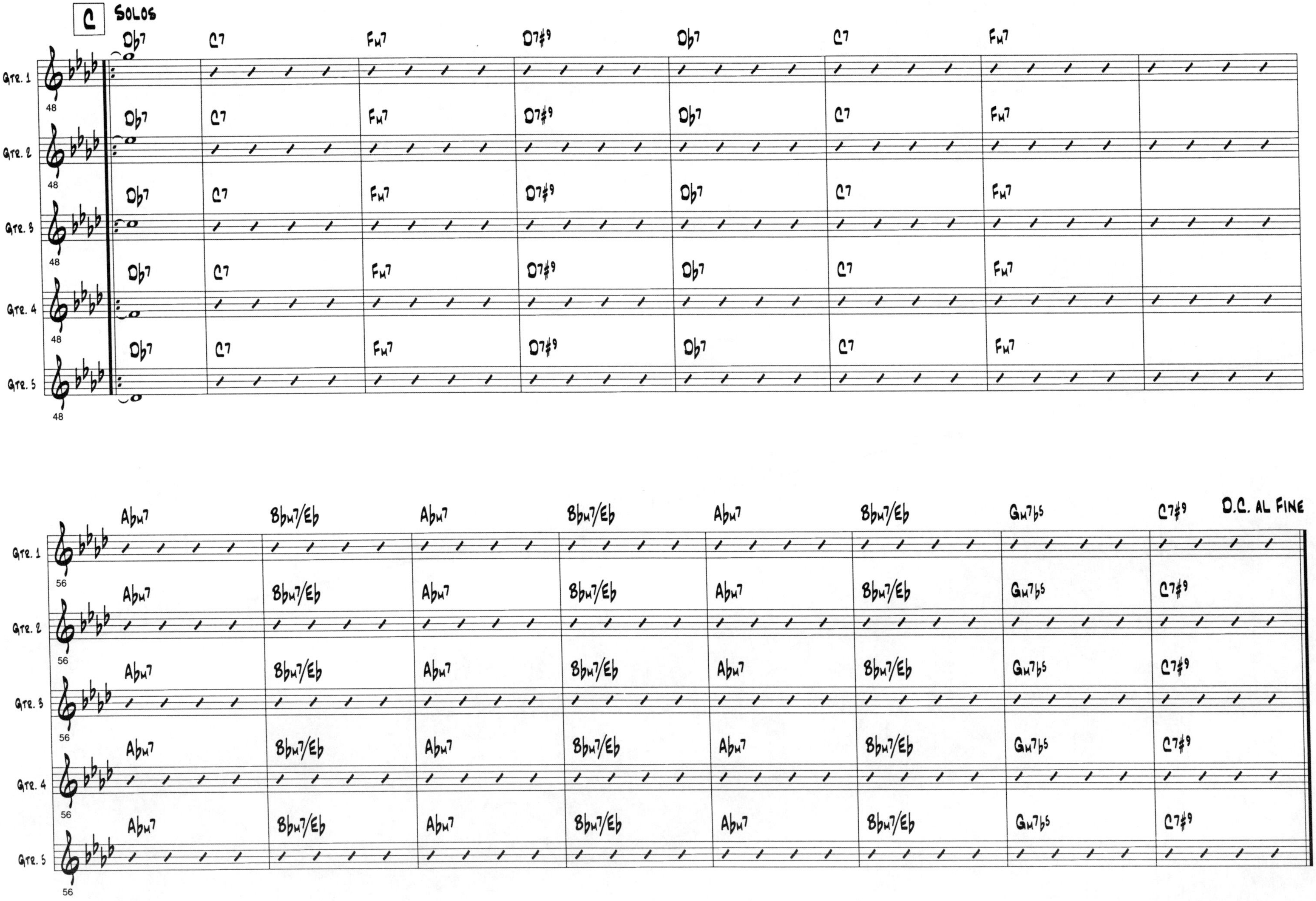
C
SOLOS
Gtr. 1
Gtr. 2
Gtr. 3
Gtr. 4
Gtr. 5
48
Db7 C7 Fm7 D7#9 Db7 C7 Fm7
56
Abm7 Bbm7/Eb Abm7 Bbm7/Eb Abm7 Bbm7/Eb Gm7b5 C7#9
D.C. AL FINE